Support for Education

CHARITY & PHILANTHROPY
UNLEASHED

Tammy Gagne

Mitchell Lane
PUBLISHERS
P.O. Box 196
Hockessin, DE 19707

Conquering Disease
Emergency Aid
Environmental Protection
Helping Children with Life-Threatening Medical Issues
Helping Our Veterans
Preserving Human Rights Around the World
The Quest to End World Hunger
Support for Education

Copyright © 2015 by Mitchell Lane Publishers

All rights reserved. No part of this book may be reproduced without written permission from the publisher. Printed and bound in the United States of America.

PUBLISHER'S NOTE: The facts in this book have been thoroughly researched. Documentation of such research can be found on pages 44–45. While every possible effort has been made to ensure accuracy, the publisher will not assume liability for damages caused by inaccuracies in the data, and makes no warranty on the accuracy of the information contained herein.

The Internet sites referenced herein were active as of the publication date. Due to the fleeting nature of some web sites, we cannot guarantee that they will all be active when you are reading this book.

Printing 1 2 3 4 5 6 7 8 9

Library of Congress Cataloging-in-Publication Data
Gagne, Tammy.
  Support for education / by Tammy Gagne.
     pages cm. — (Charity and philanthropy unleashed)
  Includes bibliographical references and index.
  ISBN 978-1-61228-577-1 (library bound)
  1. Children with social disabilities—Education—Cross-cultural studies—Juvenile literature. 2. Educational assistance—Cross-cultural studies—Juvenile literature. 3. Charities—Cross-cultural studies—Juvenile literature. I. Title.
LC4065.G34 2014
371.826′94—dc23
                                           2014006926

eBook ISBN: 9781612286150

PBP

Contents

Introduction 5
CHAPTER 1
   THE POWER OF ONE 6
   It Takes All of Us 13
CHAPTER 2
   SCHOOL BOYS AND GIRLS 14
   Boys Falling Behind 21
CHAPTER 3
   FINDING REFUGE—AND EDUCATION 22
   Starting Over 27
CHAPTER 4
   OFF THE STREETS AND INTO SCHOOL 28
   Running Away Creates New Problems 33
CHAPTER 5
   CLOSER TO HOME 34
   Kids Helping Kids 41
What You Can Do To Help 42
Chapter Notes 43
Further Reading 44
   Books 44
   On the Internet 44
   Works Consulted 44
Glossary 46
Index 47

Introduction

Going to school every day is a fact of life for most children. Many of these kids truly love learning. They look forward to getting up each morning and heading to school. For them school is a place where they learn about new things, spend time with their friends, and take part in extracurricular activities like sports or clubs. Some kids may not love or even like school. Even the ones who do enjoy school might joke about dreading Monday mornings or hoping for snow days in the winter. Whether you enjoy learning or not, one thing is almost certain: As a student, you likely take your education for granted.

Imagine for a moment not having a school. Sure, the idea of not having to go to school might sound like total freedom at first. No homework to do, no tests to study for, no teachers telling you what to do all the time. But what would happen if you didn't have those teachers? Without school you wouldn't be able to learn the things you need to know to survive as you get older. Getting a job to pay for food, housing, and transportation is much more difficult without a high school diploma. If you want to get a high-paying job, you will also need a college degree.

Getting an education isn't an easy task for many children in the world today. In some areas going to school isn't even an option. Poverty, discrimination, and war are just a few of the problems that get in the way of schooling in underdeveloped countries. For children in these areas, school is just a dream. Numerous organizations throughout the world are working to make that dream a reality for as many kids as possible.

CHAPTER 1
The Power of One

Miracle Pierre. At first his name seems almost like a cruel joke. He was born in the mid-1980s in Haiti, the poorest country in the world. About 80 percent of the people in Haiti live on less than $2 a day.[1] One of seven children, Pierre was among this majority. His father died when Pierre was just a baby, leaving him with an unpromising future. But in 2002, another man would enter his life, turning his bleak reality into an opportunity.

Roger Williams was born in Waukesha County, Wisconsin, decades before young Pierre. At the age of fifty-seven, Williams traveled to Haiti to do humanitarian work with a group called Haiti Allies. One Friday while working in a home for the destitute and dying, he noticed a teenager hanging around. He struck up a conversation with the boy and invited him to join in helping the people at the home.

Williams then asked the teen why he wasn't in school. Pierre explained that getting an education in Haiti was a difficult task. Public schools were not nearly as common in Haiti as they were in other parts of the world. And private schools required something that Pierre did not have—money. He wanted to go to school, but it just wasn't an option for him.

Pierre told his new friend about his difficult life the best he could. But he didn't know much English. His native language was Creole.

Before the end of the day, Pierre asked Williams where he would be on Monday. He shared that he would be helping out at a nearby orphanage. When Williams arrived at the door at the beginning of the new week, he found Pierre was already there. "I

Since 2010, the Clinton Foundation has raised $34 million to help the people of Haiti. Parts of the funds are being used to enhance education. Former US President Bill Clinton visited the school Union Des Apotres in Port-au-Prince in 2014 to observe the work that teachers and students are doing there.

Many people lost their lives in the earthquake that struck Haiti in 2010. In the city of Jacmel, hundreds of people were killed. Those who survived were left to deal with widespread destruction.

invited him to join me in working with the kids, and he did," remembers Williams.[2] He also recalls being very impressed with the young man. Pierre was intelligent and determined. Williams thought that he deserved the chance to go to school.

He decided to ask Haiti Allies founder Bryan Sirchio to help him make this happen. He knew that the group had a program that matched Hatian students with American sponsors. Williams didn't mention the conversation to Pierre, however. He didn't want to get his young friend's hopes up in case it didn't work out. But like Pierre, Williams was quite determined.

THE POWER OF ONE

A few weeks later the plan was in place. Pierre received a very important letter from the United States. But neither he nor his mother could read it. They ended up seeking help from Guy Morelus, the coordinator of Haiti Allies in Port-au-Prince. Morelus quickly translated, explaining that Pierre was going to get to go to school, thanks to Roger Williams and his wife Kristi. The couple would be sponsoring the young man's education.

Williams returned to Haiti in 2009 on another special mission. This time he made the trip specifically to visit his young friend who had just graduated from high school. "It was my way to help celebrate," Williams says.[3] Both he and Pierre cried when they saw each other once again.

Pierre didn't stop at getting his high school diploma. He went on to earn a two-year college degree while working part-time at a local bank. In January of 2010, a devastating earthquake rocked the island country. Pierre had been inside the bank just five minutes before the quake began. His timing may have saved his life. Many people who remained inside were killed when the building collapsed a short time later.

Following the quake Sirchio and his Haiti Allies traveled to the country again. When he did, he met up with Pierre who asked him to deliver a gift to Williams. It was a copy of his diploma—along with the original letter that Williams had sent to Haiti so many years earlier. Pierre wanted Williams to have it.

The boy who defied the odds by getting that education he wanted so badly grew up to become a vice principal. He now works at Cite Soleil Community Elementary School in Port-au-Prince, the school where his dream of an education became a reality. Perhaps Miracle was a fitting first name for him after all.

Sometimes just one person can make a huge difference in the life of another. For Miracle Pierre that person was Roger Williams. For numerous children in Cambodia, it was an American named Jamie Amelio. Just a year after Williams made his first trip to Haiti, Amelio traveled to Cambodia. While she was touring the sites, a little girl approached her. "She asked me for a dollar,"

Chapter 1

Amelio recalls. "I asked what she wanted it for. She said school. I asked her to show me the school."[4]

Amelio was taken aback by what she saw in the classrooms. Up to ten students crowded around each desk. Even worse, there was no teacher. She soon discovered that students were required to pay the teacher, when there was one. Amelio decided then and there that she wanted to help.

She enlisted the help of her husband who worked for Dell in Singapore. The first thing they did was send much-needed school supplies to the impoverished nation. The Amelios then took on an even greater project: building a new school. And they followed this project up with the building of more schools. By this point Amelio and the additional volunteers she had assembled had become a real organization named Caring for Cambodia.

All the construction and donations were opening up great possibilities for the children of Cambodia. But Amelio and her crew soon realized that the kids weren't the only ones in need of an education. If teachers were going to instruct children in these new schools, they had to be trained properly. Caring for Cambodia filled this need by adding a training system for people interested in working as teachers. By the time they had finished all the building and training, the organization had created a network of twenty-three schools.

The Cambodian government has since adopted many of the standards that Amelio set with her first school. Ung Savy is the superintendent and on-the-ground director for Caring for Cambodia. When he and Amelio first met, he taught English in the local schools. At first he was a little leery of this stranger who handed him a check for $2,000 to put towards creating a new school.

"I didn't even know it was a check," he admits. "I'd heard of checks, but never seen one." Savy soon learned that trusting Amelio was a smart move. Her vision turned into something amazing for Cambodian children. "It really has affected education

Sometimes it just takes one person to make a big difference. In 2003, Jamie Amelio traveled from Texas to Cambodia, where she discovered a great need for educational resources. She created a program to help Cambodian students, and in 2013, her story was published in a book she called *Graced with Orange*.

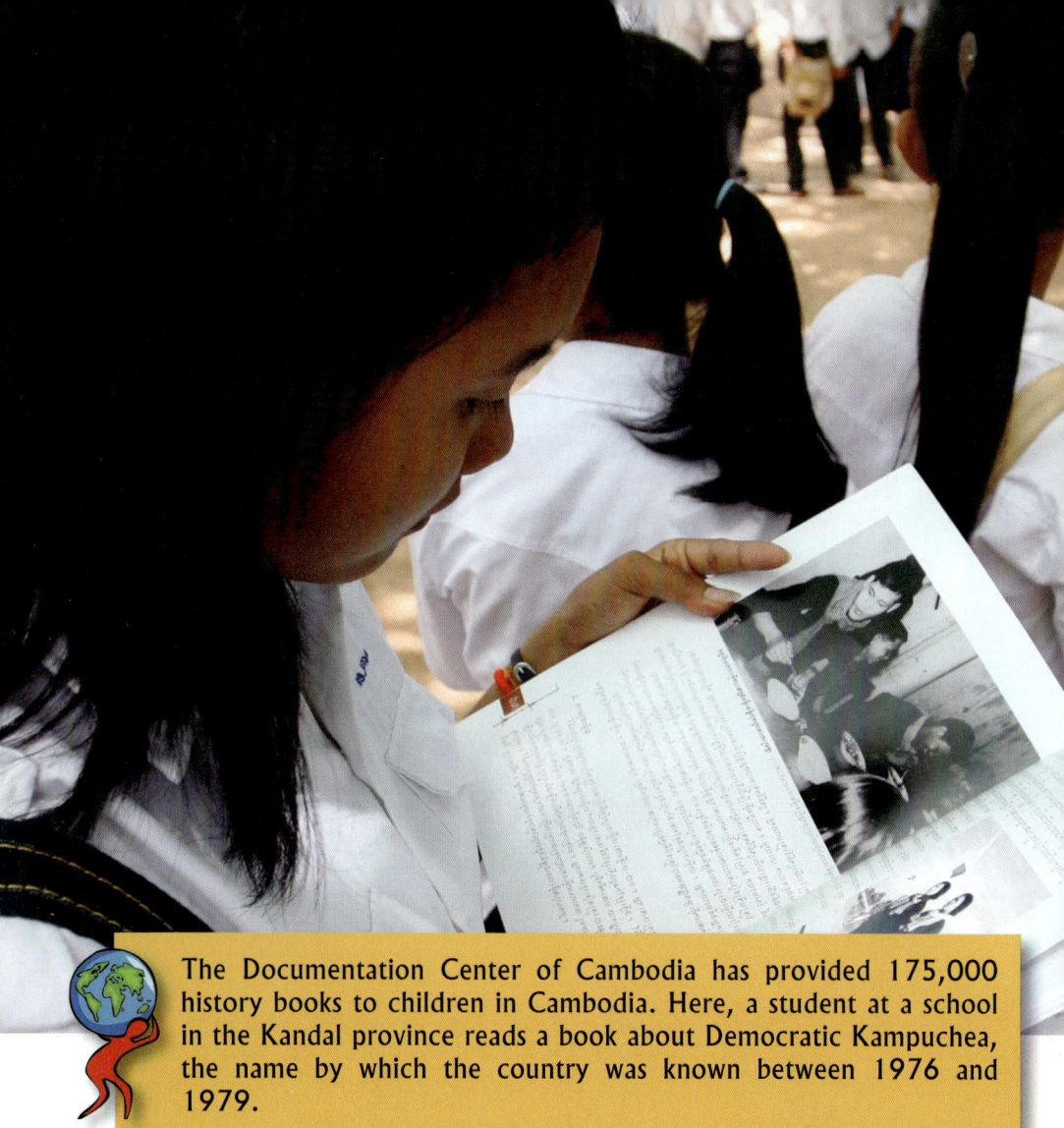

The Documentation Center of Cambodia has provided 175,000 history books to children in Cambodia. Here, a student at a school in the Kandal province reads a book about Democratic Kampuchea, the name by which the country was known between 1976 and 1979.

here," he states. "Our schools are the models in the area. Every year, nearly one thousand education officers—like teachers, principals, administrators . . . visit our schools to find out what we are doing."[5]

Savy is grateful for all the work that Caring for Cambodia has done. And he credits Amelio with the determination that made it happen. "I had never met people like her in my life," he shares. "Many people in Cambodia spent so much time to talk—hours and hours—but never help. I ask for their help, so a lot of them promise to help, but never come back. I had no idea she was so persistent."[6]

It Takes All of Us

Earl Graves Jr. is a basketball coach in the Amateur Athletic Union (AAU). He has seen firsthand that many people don't value education as much as they should. As a result of these misplaced priorities, Graves has seen some good kids miss out on some great educational—and athletic—opportunities. A few have even missed out on full scholarships worth $200,000, because they did not meet the NCAA eligibility requirements.

"We have a huge stake in the development of our students—regardless of whether we are parents or have kids attending public schools," Graves points out. "They represent our nation's future workforce and leadership. In fact, one of my personal charges as a coach is making sure that 'my boys' gain every academic advantage available to them."[7]

Graves practices what he preaches. He made a huge difference himself to a Cameroonian exchange student. The boy was a gifted athlete, but that wasn't why he took him into his home for a summer. "[H]e represented young people at their best: respectful, talented, intelligent, and fluent in three languages. Still learning to comprehend English, he initially scored poorly on his College Boards not because he wasn't smart, but rather he had not received the test preparation that is a given for privileged students in this country. As a result, this brilliant student-athlete could have been denied scholarship opportunities to attend top-notch colleges and universities. From that point on, I made it my mission to ensure that he would get the equivalent training and support that my own children received in order to be considered for scholarship and placement opportunities."[8]

Earl Graves Jr. is president and CEO of *Black Enterprise*. Graves is an advocate for making test preparation more widely available to all aspiring college students. He has seen firsthand how capable students can lose important opportunities without this help.

CHAPTER 2
School Boys and Girls

In some parts of the world, a child's educational opportunities depend largely on his or her gender. In several Arab countries, for example, girls are often denied the chance to go to school. Far more boys than girls are being educated in Sudan, Morocco, and Yemen in particular. In general the literacy rates of women in the Arab world are around 75 percent, compared to 87 percent for men.[1] This means that one out of four of the women living in Arabic-speaking countries cannot read and write their own language.

The reasons for the unequal treatment of girls vary. Certainly, economics plays a part. In the poorest countries there are fewer schools. This means that children must travel long distances to attend classes. Once there, the kids are often crammed into classrooms of one hundred students or more. In areas that are in the midst of a conflict or civil war, such as Syria, many parents choose not to send their kids for fear of their safety. But none of this explains why more boys are in school. Maybe parents are more fearful for their daughters' safety than for the safety of their sons. Maybe.

A more likely reason is that religion and culture are playing an even bigger part in denying girls the right to education. In Yemen, for example, many parents feel it is wrong for girls to attend classes with boys. Some even disapprove of girls having a male teacher. In Jordan, the problem isn't getting girls into school, but keeping them there. It is surprisingly common for girls to drop out of high school to get married in this country. Parents often put great pressure on their daughters to marry young.

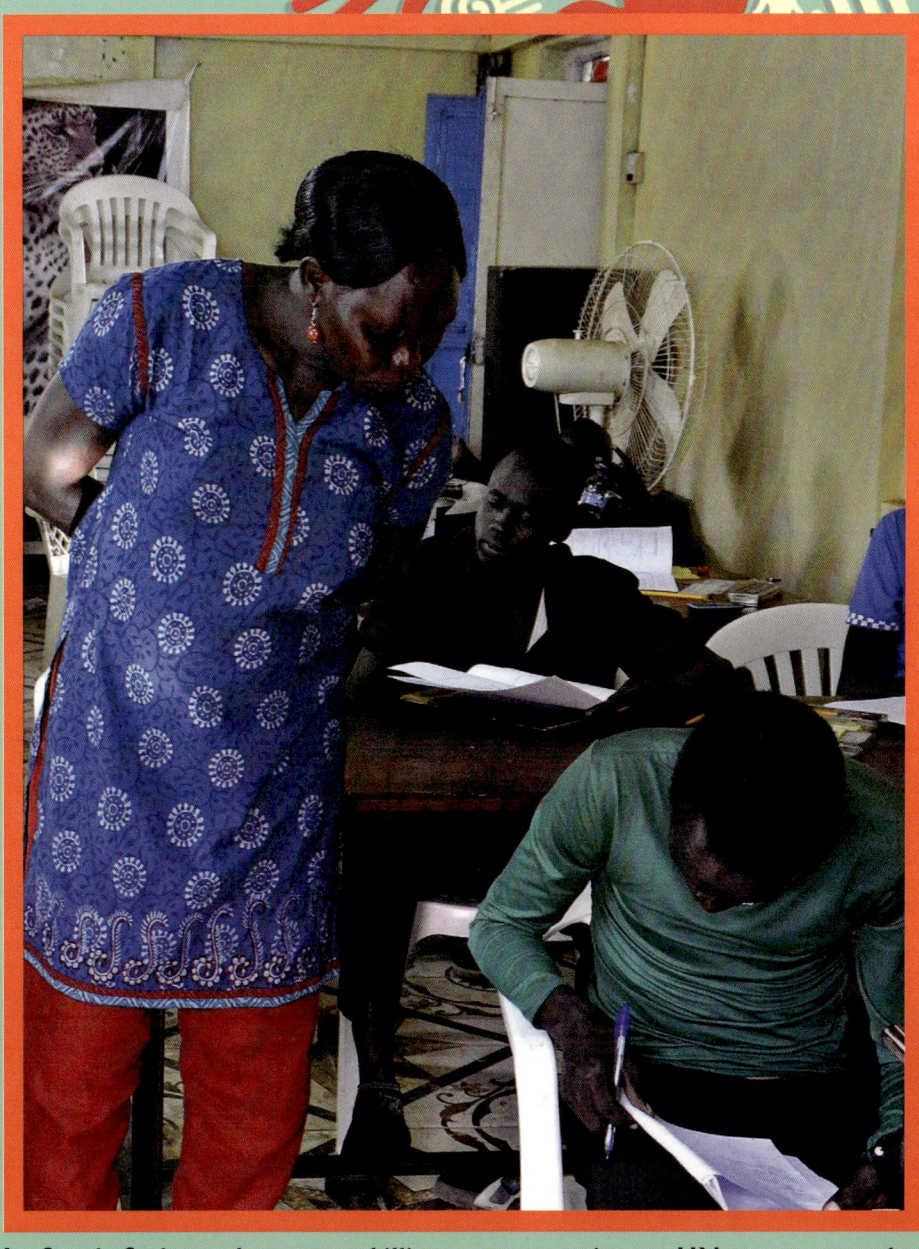

In South Sudan, where mass killings are occurring, a UN envoy says that many of the soldiers fighting in the conflicts are children. As a result many families have fled the area to avoid the terrible violence. But new problems are waiting for those who enter refugee camps in nearby countries. As many as one hundred thousand people were living in these crowded facilities by early 2014. The United Nations Mission compound in Juba, South Sudan, is working to help families there by providing education to many of the displaced children.

Malala Yousafzai has received international attention for her activism in support of education for girls. Because she spoke out, she was shot by the Taliban on her way to school when she was just fifteen years old. But the brave Pakistani girl continued to fight for her right to receive an education.

SCHOOL BOYS AND GIRLS

Many Middle Eastern families don't even consider sending their daughters to school, because they think it would be a waste of time. Men dominate the job market in this part of the world. Girls who do finish school have a very hard time finding employment. Ironically, many of them end up becoming teachers. Both the pay they receive and their working conditions are often horrible. Worse yet, these teachers often aren't trained properly, setting even more female students up for failure.

Girls in this region of the world become caught in a cycle that denies them voices in their own futures. When girls are not able to go to school, they cannot learn about their government—or about the governments of more progressive countries. Without a basic knowledge of their government, they have little hope to change the very laws that keep them from becoming educated in the first place.

Sometimes even progress gets in the way of education for girls in the Middle East. In 2012, an education department in the north of Pakistan merged two of its schools into one. The goal of this project was to create a better educational setting for students. But for the female students of Kaccha, a village in Hassan Abdal, the change meant an end to their education. Parents in this region feel that allowing boys and girls to go to school together goes against the teachings of Islam. The parents in the village responded to the change by keeping their daughters home instead of sending them to the new school.

Should a person's religion prevent her from receiving an education? It is important to respect all religions. But what some people see as religion, others see as an excuse for discrimination. The education department in Pakistan claims the schools had to be merged because there were not enough teachers to keep two schools open. But some people think that the male leaders of the country are happier with the idea of girls remaining at home.

While many of the biggest barriers to education for girls are found halfway across the world, certain gender divisions also exist in the United States. American girls don't have to fight for

Chapter 2

the right to attend school, of course. But it is apparent that boys and girls are often drawn to different fields of study in the states. In Connecticut, for example, the majority of students studying the STEM fields (science, technology, engineering, and math) are male. On the national level, of students who graduate with engineering degrees, only 17 percent of them are female. Even fewer professional engineers are female—just 11 percent.[2]

Many educators think that the reason for these low numbers is that young girls are getting the wrong messages about women's roles in the workforce. Paige Rasid is the marketing and operations manager for the Connecticut Technology Council. She explains, "They're making those choices [about math and science courses] at thirteen, fourteen, and fifteen years old. That really does determine what their life will look like as they finish up college."[3]

Some institutions have set up programs to even out the numbers of their male and female STEM students. St. Joseph College in West Hartford, Connecticut, for instance, has created a program called GO-GIRL, which targets female students in middle school. Sarah Higbie, a biology professor at the college reveals, "That's the make-or-break year for girls going into science fields."[4]

GO-GIRL stands for Gaining Options: Girls Investigate Real Life, a fitting title for the hands-on exposure that the program offers. Meeting on Saturdays, project members take part in all kinds of scientific studies. One week they might learn about statistics; the next they may extract DNA from fruit.

In 2009, Central Connecticut State University hosted its first Girls in Technology Expo. The all-day event offers workshops and exhibits in a variety of science-related subjects. Girls can learn how bicycle gears work or how to use computer animation programs to produce short films. About one hundred girls in all typically attend the program. One recent participant was Aleyah Seabrook, a seventh-grader who wants to be a forensic scientist when she grows up.

SCHOOL BOYS AND GIRLS

Wendy Holforty is the outreach chair for the Women's Influence Network at NASA's Ames Research Center. She is seen here high-fiving students taking part in the competition.

In order to help her reach her goals, she is working with a mentor. The middle-schooler knows that having a female role model will be a wonderful resource as she works towards her career goals. "I feel it's harder [for women]," Seabrook shares. "It's more of a man's world than a woman's world."[5]

Fortunately, Connecticut isn't the only state working to increase female enrollment in STEM education. The programs also don't end at the middle school level. Radford University's College of Science and Technology in Virginia hosts an annual event called the Summer Bridge program. This week-long experience is designed for high school sophomore, junior, and senior girls interested in science, technology, and math. The students stay right on campus for the entire week, working with actual university professors. These instructors teach the girls

Colleges and universites across the United States offer summer bridge programs to high school students. Here, female students taking part in one such program at Central Missouri State University are seen touring the campus's radio station with its program director, Jon Hart.

about a wide range of subjects including medicine, forensics, and even space exploration.

Penelope W. Kyle is the president of Radford University. Addressing the seventy-eight young women who attended the 2013 Summer Bridge event, Kyle stated, "You are at the perfect point to decide if you're going to be one of these young women who creates and seeks your own opportunities. I hope, whether it's a year from now, two years from now, or ten years from now, you look back on this week at Radford University and you say 'that was it. That was when that thought was planted in my mind. That was when I got there with all those other young women and realized I could compete with them in the STEM disciplines.'"[6]

Boys Falling Behind

British journalist Ally Fogg wants to make sure that boys aren't forgotten when it comes to education. "There are now one-third more female than male students applying for university," he says of his home country. "Women are now more likely to be accepted for higher education than men are even to apply. Some of this can be accounted for by school exam results—girls have been outperforming boys at A-level for many years, but the gap in university applications and admissions is actually wider than the results gap. It would appear that many young men who could apply for university are opting not to."[7]

Fogg points out that the push for more girls to pursue education has been both necessary and worthwhile. But he sees another gap between the genders opening up. "I am parent to two school-aged boys, the elder of which enters secondary school next year. He thinks he is doing pretty well because he mostly gets higher marks than the other boys in his class. He is entirely resigned to, and comfortable with the knowledge, that he lags far behind several of the girls. I don't know where this comes from, but I'm pretty sure it wasn't from home. Nor would I blame individual teachers at his school, because I have no doubt the same thought patterns are being played out by boys across the country, perhaps across the world. . . . Sooner or later we have to face up to the need for similar efforts to energise and inspire boys."[8]

Many boys are trailing girls both in grades and in college applications.

CHAPTER 3
Finding Refuge— and Education

Many children in the poorest countries of the world dream of being able to go to school one day. For young refugees from war-torn regions, though, this dream seems ever further from reach. With no country to call their own, their families must focus first and foremost on survival. In these cases education often falls to the bottom of the priority list.

The United Nations estimates the number of refugees in the world today at more than fifteen million.[1] When we take a closer look, we discover that an overwhelming number of these displaced people are children. For example, more than two million people have fled the country of Syria in recent years, moving into the border regions of Lebanon, Turkey, Iraq, Jordan, and Egypt. More than half of these refugees are under the age of eighteen.[2]

Save the Children is an international organization that helps children who are facing difficult situations in countries around the world. Miled Abou Jaoude is the emergency coordinator for Save the Children in Lebanon. He points out, "The biggest problem is the language."[3] Syrian children come to the area speaking only Arabic, but some Lebanese classes are taught in either English or French. Syrian refugees also often have to repeat grades they had already completed back home. Experts say this is because the Lebanese school system is more advanced and difficult.

To make matters worse, the very nature of refugee life means that many of these children have spent more than a year out of school before coming to Lebanon. Although Lebanese schools readily accept Syrian students, many parents do not realize this

Here, a twelve-year-old Syrian girl named Aziza (right) is seen dancing and singing. Today she lives in Lebanon, but for two years she and her family were displaced in Syria due to the conflict there. Organizations like War Child and UNICEF helped Aziza make it back to school after the life-changing move.

German First Lady Daniela Schadt has made education part of her focus. Here, she visits with a Syrian family who left their home in Damascus to move to Amman, Jordan. Schadt works with UNICEF to help provide aid for refugee families like this one.

fact until registration deadlines have passed. As a result children often have to wait several more months before getting back to learning. And the longer they wait, the harder it can be to adjust to the new setting. Many choose to start working instead of finishing their education.

Syrian families do not have to pay for their children to attend school, but this doesn't mean there is no cost involved. Some families rely on their children to help put food on the table. For those who can get by without their children working, the cost of transportation to school is often too expensive. Because students may have to travel a great distance to reach their school, some parents also worry for their kids' safety.

For refugee children in some parts of the world, school isn't an actual building. Instead, it is merely a gathering that takes place in or near refugee camps. For these kids a classroom might be any empty space that the teacher and students can use for a few hours. The iTemba Study Centre in the Berea neighborhood of Johannesburg, South Africa, is one such school. About 140 refugee children meet up each day on the first floor of an office building to take part in this project.

FINDING REFUGE—AND EDUCATION

Judith Manjoro was an unemployed teacher from Zimbabwe who realized that these kids needed her help. She noticed numerous refugee children playing in the streets and local parks of Berea during school hours. Many of them came from families who couldn't afford to send them to school. Others had faced resistance when trying to enroll. The schools had asked them to produce identification and other paperwork that they simply didn't have. Manjoro and several other community workers decided to create the iTemba Study Centre for these kids. It serves students from preschool to eighth grade.

Duduzile Zulu is a fifteen-year-old refugee from Zimbabwe who attends the program. "It's a good school," she says, "but we don't have enough supplies." Since the refugee school doesn't offer classes beyond the eighth grade, Zulu will need to join another school soon. This change may not even be possible for her. "I don't have a birth certificate," she explains, "and my mum can't get time off work to go to [the Department of] Home Affairs."[4]

The Centre for Education Rights and Transformation at the University of Johannesburg performed a study that uncovered some upsetting information. South African schools often demand paperwork that is not legally required to enroll refugee students. Ivor Baatjes, one of the study researchers, is just one of the people who think this is wrong. He points out that many school administrators are unaware that South African law entitles *every child* to an education. "Even for children of undocumented migrants, children have the right to be in school and nothing should be a barrier," he states.[5]

Many refugees themselves are unaware of their rights. This lack of knowledge makes it even easier for some schools to discriminate against students from other countries. For example, South African law states that public school is free to everyone. But some schools are demanding that students pay fees for attendance nonetheless.

Discrimination seems to be at work at every level. Many refugee children are made to feel unwelcome by the other kids in

Chapter 3

public schools. Worse yet, even some South African teachers are guilty of xenophobia, the technical term for the fear or dislike of people from other countries. This poor treatment leaves many refugees like those in the iTemba Study Centre afraid to move on to public school.

Sixteen-year-old Antonia Tshili is an iTemba student who has faced discrimination in South Africa's public school system. The refugee from Zimbabwe says, "They treat people equally [at iTemba]. At the [public] school there is this thing that Zimbabweans should go back to their country; they bullied me."[6]

Another project that helps refugee students on their path to education in South Africa is Three2Six. This program takes place at Sacred Heart College in Observatory, a suburb of Cape Town. When South African students head home in the afternoon, refugee children arrive to begin their schooling. Like iTemba, Three2Six is a temporary solution. It is meant to bridge the gaps between the refugees and a more traditional education. The goal is to prepare these children for entrance into South Africa's public school system.

One of the biggest advantages of the Three2Six program is that many of the teachers are refugees themselves. This fact is often very helpful in terms of language and culture. The kids can use their time at Three2Six to learn English in an environment where many of them feel more comfortable. Entering mainstream schools still may not be easy for them, but programs like iTemba and Three2Six definitely give them a better chance at integration when that time arrives.

South Africa's Department of Education does not recognize either program. For this reason the programs receive no public funding. Instead, they rely on money from various charities and other organizations. The iTemba program charges a small fee to families who can afford to pay it. This fee helps cover the costs of renting the classroom space and paying teachers. But a large number of parents simply cannot pay it.

Starting Over

The city of Palmerston North, New Zealand, is home to dozens of students who are former refugees. They come from various places, but they have something very important in common. All of them have been given a second chance in this new land.

Eighteen-year-old Laibar Boli was born in a Thai refugee camp that her parents called home for twenty-three years. They had fled Myanmar (also known as Burma) because of the fighting between Burmese nationals and the Karen ethnic minority group there. They remained in the camp for many years out of fear. "We did not have the right to leave the camp because then the Thai army would arrest us," she explains. Although she doesn't remember everything about the camp, she knows that her opportunities there were severely limited. "We didn't have education over there," she adds.[7]

When Boli was eleven, her family was allowed to move to New Zealand. Today she lives in Palmerston North, where she attends Freyberg High School. She counts her freedom and the opportunity for education among her blessings.

Sarah Nzamba is also eighteen. In 2009, she and her brother came to Palmerston North from the Democratic Republic of the Congo. When she arrived in New Zealand, she was most surprised by the diversity. "It was very scary but awesome. I had to learn a new language and the culture and stuff, it was kind of hard. . . . People were telling me about New Zealand—that it was really beautiful—but until I arrived I thought it was only white people here, which is what I was told. . . . I didn't know there were other cultures living here but I moved here and found there were many."[8]

Thousands of people from Myanmar live in Thailand's refugee camps. Here, one of these young women (left) is being treated for malaria.

In June 2013, Freyberg High School celebrated World Refugee Day. Students who had come to Palmerston North as refugees got to share a bit of their culture with their classmates. The refugees dressed in their national costumes to honor the family members and friends who had been lost or left behind. They also took part in a tree planting ceremony that symbolized the new life they had begun in New Zealand.

CHAPTER 4
Off the Streets and into School

About 168 million children throughout the world go to work each day instead of attending school.[1] Some of these kids have actual jobs so they can earn money for their families. Other kids "work" by taking care of their younger brothers or sisters for their parents while they perform their own jobs. The problem with this way of life is that it keeps the poor in professions that pay very little. When children cannot go to school, they cannot get better jobs than their parents had. Instead, they merely repeat the cycle of working hard for next to nothing, and having their own children who must eventually do the same.

Other children work because they have no families to take care of them. Some of these kids have run away from home; others were abandoned by their parents. Nowhere are these problems greater than in the country of India. As many as eighteen million kids live on the streets in India.[2] Without an address, they cannot register for school. Even if they could register, other problems—like transportation—would quickly arise.

Satender Sharma was once one of those street kids. He ran away from home when he was just eleven years old. His story is a horrific one. "My father used to [beat] up all our family," he explains. "He is taking alcohol. One day he [beat] my mom very badly, and he killed her."[3]

Desperate to escape from his abusive situation, Sharma headed for the nearest railway station. He then snuck onto a train that was headed to New Delhi. He arrived in the city all alone with

Many children living in India face a harsh reality. The slums, like this one near Mumbai, are filled with families who have next to nothing. Living in tiny shacks with numerous people in each room, they have every right to feel sorry for themselves. But many people from this region have responded to their situation with hope and hard work instead of despair. Some people have opened shops or other small businesses. Many of them have also sent their children to school so they can learn valuable skills that will improve their own lives.

The Salaam Baalak Trust helps young people living on the streets of New Delhi. The group provides runaways with a place to stay, medical care, and education.

no money. He quickly learned how to survive, but just barely. Forced to beg, borrow, and steal, school wasn't even on his mind.

"Boys, living on the street, they have many jobs to do," shares Sharma, "pick-pocketing, begging, . . . cleaning cars, shoe shining, and selling rubbish. Doing these jobs," as he calls them, "they can earn more than two hundred rupees per day." This amount is equal to about $4.50. But it is more than double what most people in India live on every day.[4]

OFF THE STREETS AND INTO SCHOOL

Another problem soon besets these homeless youngsters: If they don't spend the money they make, someone will almost certainly steal it from them. Older kids, crafty adults, and even corrupt police officers often force street kids to hand over whatever money they have. The kids' solution is to spend everything they make each day.

You might think they would spend a good part of their money on food. But most of the kids eat their meals at Sikh temples. These religious temples often feed the homeless. When a free meal can't be found, many street kids simply steal their food from railway stations. They then spend their money on entertainment like movies, video games, and drugs. Movies serve a dual purpose on Fridays. Kids can sleep on and off in the theaters while watching a Bollywood triple-feature.

The Salaam Baalak Trust is a group that helps kids who are living on the streets in New Delhi. A social worker from Salaam Baalak, which means "hello, street kid," reached out to Sharma, helping him turn his life around. It was a slow process for him, though. He spent six months at the group's community center before he trusted anyone enough to share his story with them. The center offers street kids a place to stay while they receive schooling and medical care. Once a child feels ready, he or she can then move into one of Salaam Baalak's five homes. For these kids, the only way to create access to education is to solve their bigger problem of homelessness first.

For Indian children lucky enough to have families and homes to call their own, opening doors to education is somewhat simpler. In a country with such a high population, though, getting the poorest children to school still isn't easy. The Ahmedabad Municipal Corporation decided to try a different approach: taking the school to the children instead of vice versa. The group has created a school on wheels in the form of seven vans that travel around the slums of Ahmedabad, located in western India.

Each van is equipped with a generator, a computer, and an LCD television with DVD player. It can work with twenty-two

Chapter 4

students at any one time. Each van makes two daily stops, one in the morning and one in the afternoon. The goal of the program is to get kids interested in education. Once the children show a desire to continue learning, they can then work on moving them to mainstream schools in the area.

The idea of a mobile school wasn't a new one. In 2009, the Lok Vikas Evam Anusandhan Trust also began a school-on-wheels program with the help of the United Nations Children's Fund (UNICEF). This program operates in Indore, about 250 miles east of Ahmedabad. Bela Jain is the program's coordinator. She shares, "Two teachers trained in multi-level and multi-grade teaching, along with one helper, visit two construction sites daily and teach the children fundamentals of four basic subjects—mathematics, English, Hindi, and environment."[5]

Like the Ahmedabad Municipal Corporation's vans, the buses offer education without pressure. Students are free to attend whenever they want. They do not need to take part every single day. As long as there is enough room, all kids who want to participate are welcome at any time. The teachers do their best to make learning fun.

Jain adds, "We also organise cultural programmes and competitions for the children and teach them India's history and patriotic songs. These activities increase their interest in attending the school."[6] Since its start this school on wheels has worked with over 1,500 children. Of those students, about forty have gone on to join regular schools. Clearly, the success rate hasn't been overwhelming. But to those forty students who decided to continue their education, the traveling schools have made a huge difference in their lives.

Running Away Creates New Problems

When young people run away from home, the effects are long lasting. Not having an education makes it even harder for them to get by on their own as they move into young adulthood. Cordella Hill is the executive director of Covenant House in Philadelphia, Pennsylvania. The charity provides crisis care and other services to runaways. "We have young people who have been in placement, in foster care who have 'aged out' of the system," Hill shares. "I don't want to disparage the Department of Human Services in any way, but the focus isn't on preparing these young people for independence. It starts too late; the emphasis isn't as focused as it should be, on helping these kids gain the skills needed to succeed on their own. You can no longer succeed in this society without an education or some sort of vocational skill set. I get kids at age eighteen and I ask them, 'What can you do?' and they'll say 'Well, I can rap.' I'm sorry but that's not really going to help them get a job or help me get them a job. I worry everyday about what are my kids going to do in five years."[7]

Many of the young people Hill encounters can't even fill out a job application without help. They lack the necessary reading and comprehension skills. "Even the military requires that you pass certain competency tests," Hill states. "I don't know what it's going to take to help our children in Philadelphia realize the value of education because so many of them don't see it as an avenue out. They don't see the point, they don't want to do the four years of school. I'm seeing this in an entire generation and it really makes me concerned over what's going to happen to them."[8]

No matter why young people arrive at Covenant House, the organization helps them get back on their feet.

CHAPTER 5
Closer to Home

Education isn't just a problem in other countries. Getting kids to go to and stay in school is also a challenge in many cities and towns in the United States. Certainly, the US overall is managing much better than many poor or war-torn countries. The graduation rate in the United States is close to 75 percent. This number is the highest it has been since 1973.[1] But this impressive figure also means that more than 25 percent of children are not graduating from high school.

When we take a look at specific cities, the numbers are even more startling. In our country's capital, Washington, DC, the graduation rate is just 57 percent. New York City's rate is 54 percent. One might think that it's the east coast bringing the national average down. But things are even worse in certain cities out west. Los Angeles, California, has a graduation rate of just 52 percent. The number in Albuquerque, New Mexico, is even worse: 51 percent. Milwaukee, Wisconsin, ties New York City at 54 percent. And in Detroit, Michigan, only 46 percent of students are graduating from high school.[2]

For many students it just takes one mistake to set them on a path that doesn't include finishing high school. Johnathan Hicks had never gotten into trouble until he made the mistake that changed the course of his education. He was a straight-A student with perfect attendance. He had even won several science fair awards. None of these accomplishments matter, however, when a school has a zero-tolerance policy. This means that the punishment is the same no matter what the circumstances.

Many Americans are surprised to learn just how low high school graduation rates are across the United States. In many cities the number of students earning a high school diploma accounts for little more than half the graduation-aged population.

Chapter 5

In areas where student safety has become an elevated concern, many schools have installed metal detectors. These devices help to identify weapons like guns or knives before anyone can carry them into the building. Metal detectors have been a common sight at many high schools for years. But they are new to many elementary schools, like this one in Drums, Pennsylvania.

One day near the end of his third-grade year, Hicks brought a gun onto his school bus in Savannah, Georgia. His stepfather had picked the weapon up at a flea market. Because it didn't work, his stepdad had left the weapon in a box on his nightstand, unloaded. The nine-year-old found it and thought it was a BB gun. He decided to take it on the bus to show his friends. Thankfully, no one was hurt in the incident. But the school officials would not make an exception to the rules.

When all was said and done, Hicks was sent to Scott Alternative Learning Center. The purpose of this school is to educate kids with discipline problems, learning difficulties, or both. Hicks would have to attend the alternative school for at least one year before he would even have a chance to return to his mainstream school. His mother offered to home-school him for this time period, but her request was denied.

An average day at Scott Alternative Learning Center is very different from a day at a regular school. Students from kindergarten through high school arrive at Scott each morning much like they did at their previous schools. But as soon as they walk through the door, the differences are striking. Students must line up, remove their shoes and belts, and empty their pockets. Their coats get locked in a special room for the rest of the day. Next, an officer waves a handheld metal detector over each student to make sure that he or she isn't hiding any weapons. Kids who are deemed a minimal risk to others must wear white shirts. Kids who are thought to be a higher risk to others must wear blue or yellow.

Hicks's mother, Aishia Hicks-Groover, says the experience was a horrible one for her son. It began with him having to ride on a bus with eleventh and twelfth graders. When his mom found out that some of these older kids fought and did drugs at the bus stop, she started getting up early to drive him to school herself. But he soon began to fear going to school nonetheless, crying each morning. The child who used to love school could now barely focus on learning. He explains, "I kept thinking about what I did and how I wasn't supposed to do that. I was sad and mad. When you do something bad, bad things happen to you."[3]

Hicks-Groover shares that she wasn't the only one who thought her son was in the wrong place. "I even had a counselor

Chapter 5

at the school tell me once 'your son doesn't really belong here, but most of these [other] kids are lifers.' Instead of labeling kids 'lifers' I think schools like this should be helping kids turn their lives around. Society just throws them away at such an early age."[4]

Hicks was luckier than many kids struggling to make it through school in Savannah. He was able to make it through this difficult year and return to mainstream classes. He is now in a public middle school. Hopefully he will stay in school long enough to graduate in a few years.

Joel Rosch is a senior research scholar at Duke University's Center for Child and Family Policy. He warns, "It's important that we not paint all alternative programs with one broad brush. In some cases, a smaller alternative setting where adults can work hard to prevent negative peer influences, can be a good thing; it can give some kids a second chance."[5]

Perhaps a better way to approach the problem, though, is by giving kids a better *first* chance. Marty Duckenfield is the spokesperson for the National Dropout Prevention Center. She explains, "People don't often think about preschool as [an element of] dropout prevention. They think of the surly high school kid with behavior problems—but it goes back to other issues, and one is early childhood education."[6]

Before they can work on preschool programs, though, some school districts must first make kindergarten a bigger priority. For example, did you know that kids living in Alaska, Idaho, Michigan, New Jersey, New York, and Pennsylvania do not have to attend school until first grade? Although many cities in these states offer kindergarten classes to their residents, none of these six states require their school districts to do so.[7]

Help is also needed at the first-grade level. A national program called Reading Recovery is working on this problem. The group helps first-graders who are having trouble learning to read and write. Reading Recovery has been working with young children in the United States since 1984, helping more than two million

CLOSER TO HOME

David Valle is a teacher at the Fischer School, which is part of Orange County Juvenile Hall in California. Specializing in math and science, he helps young people at the facility earn their high school diplomas.

kids in the process. Eighty percent of the kids who use this valuable resource can read at their grade level by the time they finish the program.[8]

Kyle Snow is the director of the Center for Applied Research at the National Association for the Education of Young Children.

Many experts think the key to getting children to stay in school is getting them into school early. Kids who learn to read at a young age often have an easier time learning other subjects. Likewise, kids who struggle with reading often find school more difficult.

His work has taught him how important it is to focus on today. He says the best way to help a child learn is, "to understand where the child is, where they are heading, and how to get from point A to point B. It's not based on what the child will need to do in third grade, but what they did yesterday, what they need to do tomorrow, and how to get there."[9]

Kids Helping Kids

Waynflete School in Portland, Maine, has created a mentoring program that allows older kids to help younger ones. Through two different after-school programs, Waynflete students are working with kids at nearby Reiche Elementary. A pair of students, one from each school, spends time together for twenty weeks, taking part in both recreational and educational activities. The goals are for the older kids to show the younger ones how to lead and succeed by creating a variety of developmental assets.

David Vaughan, a biology teacher at Waynflete, is the program's coordinator. "There are forty developmental assets," he explains. They include self-confidence, hope, and having people in the community who care. "The more developmental assets the students have, the less likely they will engage in risky behavior and the more likely they will thrive."[10]

Ali Schklair is a Waynflete student who mentors a younger girl. She admits that the work is not always easy. "When I started the program, I naively thought I would be changing my buddy's life," she recalls, "but as the years have passed I have noticed that I had to work extra hard to gain her trust just to relate to her on a friendship level."[11]

Vaughan shares that all the hard work is well worth the effort, though. "The beauty is in the seeing," he states. "For some, the going can sometimes be slow, but the light that you see in the faces of little ones when they see their mentor come to Reiche is very tangible."[12]

Student mentoring programs are a valuable educational resource.

WHAT YOU CAN DO TO HELP

Even though you are still in the process of finishing your own education, you can help support education for others. Here are just a few of the ways that you can make a difference in someone else's future:

The most important thing you can do to help support education is finishing your own. You might not even realize it, but you may be a role model for a younger person already. By staying in school and making school a priority in your own life, you show others the importance of doing the same.

If you are interested in helping a younger person you don't already know, ask a teacher if there is already a mentoring program in place at your school. If there is not, ask if you could help start one.

Ask a teacher to help you start a virtual pen pal program at your school. Kids who are learning English in other countries need to practice reading and writing the language. What better way than speaking with American children or teens online? Be sure to ask for an adult's help, though. You should never talk to anyone you don't know online without having an adult make sure it's safe.

Consider volunteering some of your time to an organization that teaches English as a Second Language (ESL). You don't have to join the Peace Corps to find people who could use your knowledge—although that could be a wonderful goal for the future! In the meantime, though, an after-school program might be able to put you to work practicing English with ESL students by doing fun things like reading or playing games.

Consider donating books that you do not plan to read again to an educational program in your area. Donations such as notebooks, pencils and pens, and other learning supplies are also useful to many educational programs.

CHAPTER NOTES

Chapter 1: The Power of One
1. Michael B. Sauter, Alexander E. M. Hess, and Samuel Weigley, Fox Business, "The 10 Poorest Countries in the World," September 14, 2012.
2. Doug Moe, *Wisconsin State Journal*, "Miracle of Education Thriving in Haiti," November 16, 2012.
3. Ibid.
4. Michael Barnes, *Austin American-Statesman*, "Texan With a Vision Creates a School District—from Scratch—in Cambodia," July 14, 2013.
5. Ibid.
6. Ibid.
7. Earl G. Graves Jr., *Black Enterprise*, "We Must Make Our Kids' Education Our Top Priority," September 2012, Volume 43, Issue 2, p. 12.
8. Ibid.

Chapter 2: School Boys and Girls
1. UNESCO Institute for Statistics, The World Bank, "Literacy Rate, Adult Female (% of Females Ages 15 and Above)." http://data.worldbank.org/indicator/SE.ADT.LITR.FE.ZS
2. Jodie Mozdzer, *The Courant*, "Array of Science Programs Targets Middle School Girls," April 7, 2009.
3. Ibid.
4. Ibid.
5. Ibid.
6. Chad Osborne, Radford University, "Summer Bridge Inspires STEM Education for High School Girls," July 15, 2013.
7. Ally Fogg, *The Guardian*, "Education is Leaving Boys Behind," December 13, 2012.
8. Ibid.

Chapter 3: Finding Refuge—and Education
1. UN Refugee Agency, "Facts and Figures about Refugees." http://www.unhcr.org.uk/about-us/key-facts-and-figures.html
2. UN Refugee Agency, *Syria Regional Refugee Response*, "Regional Overview," October 7, 2013. http://data.unhcr.org/syrianrefugees/regional.php
3. IRIN, "Lebanon-Syria: No School Today—Why Syrian Refugee Children Miss Out on Education," August 8, 2012.
4. IRIN, "South Africa: Refugee Children Miss Out on School," January 31, 2012.
5. Ibid.
6. Ibid.
7. Talia Shadwell, *Manawatu Standard*, "Students Share Refugee Experience," June 28, 2013.
8. Ibid.

Chapter 4: Off the Streets and into School
1. International Labour Organization, "Child Labour." http://www.ilo.org/global/topics/child-labour/lang--en/index.htm
2. Corey Flintoff, National Public Radio, "A Strange Tourist Attraction: India's Street Kids," January 23, 2011.
3. Ibid.
4. Ibid.
5. Nupoor Rashinkar, DNA Syndication, "School Goes to Children—On Wheels," September 22, 2011.
6. Ibid.
7. Larry Miller, *The Philadelphia Tribune*, "Hidden Homeless," July 23, 2010.
8. Ibid.

Chapter 5: Closer to Home
1. Valerie Strauss, *The Washington Post*, "US High School Graduation Rate Sees Big Minority Gains—Analysis," June 6, 2013.
2. Ibid.
3. Chandra Thomas Whitfield, *Crisis*, "School Scam," Spring 2012, Volume 119, Issue 2, p. 22.
4. Ibid.
5. Ibid., p. 25.
6. Alison DeNisco, *District Administration*, "Closing Early Education Gaps for At-Risk Students," June 1, 2013, p. 36.
7. Ibid., p. 38.
8. Ibid., p. 39.
9. Ibid., p. 41.
10. Melanie Creamer, *Portland Press Herald*, "Older, Younger Kids Like Being Buddies; Mentoring Relationships Formed in After-School Programs Have Tangible Benefits for Students," March 7, 2007.
11. Ibid.
12. Ibid.

FURTHER READING

Books
Gruwell, Erin. *The Freedom Writers Diary.* New York: Broadway Books, 2009.

Hughes, Susan. *Off to Class: Incredible and Unusual Schools Around the World.* Toronto, Ontario: Turtleback Books, 2011.

Thompson, Gail L. *Up Where We Belong: Helping African American and Latino Students Rise in School and in Life.* Hoboken, NJ: Wiley, 2007.

On the Internet
Boys and Girls Clubs of America
http://www.bgca.org/Pages/index.aspx

Peace Corps
http://www.peacecorps.gov/

UNICEF
http://www.unicef.org/

Works Consulted
Barnes, Michael. "Texan With a Vision Creates a School District—from Scratch—in Cambodia." *Austin American-Statesman*, July 14, 2013.

Brock, Colin, and Nafsika Alexiadou. *Education Around the World.* New York: Bloomsbury, 2013.

Covey, Stephen R. *The Leader in Me: How Schools and Parents Around the World Are Inspiring Greatness, One Child at a Time.* New York: Free Press, 2008.

Creamer, Melanie. "Older, Younger Kids Like Being Buddies; Mentoring Relationships Formed in After-School Programs Have Tangible Benefits for Students." *Portland Press Herald*, March 7, 2007.

DeNisco, Alison. "Closing Early Education Gaps for At-Risk Students." *District Administration*, June 1, 2013.

Faisal, Safa. "Muslim Girls Struggle for Education." BBC News, September 24, 2003. http://news.bbc.co.uk/2/hi/middle_east/3130234.stm

Flintoff, Corey. "A Strange Tourist Attraction: India's Street Kids." National Public Radio, January 23, 2011. http://www.npr.org/2011/01/23/133109831/taking-a-walk-into-the-lives-of-indias-street-kids

Fogg, Ally. "Education is Leaving Boys Behind." *The Guardian*, December 13, 2012. http://www.theguardian.com/commentisfree/2012/dec/13/education-leaving-boys-behind

Graves, Earl G. Jr. "We Must Make Our Kids' Education Our Top Priority." *Black Enterprise*, September 2012, Volume 43, Issue 2, p. 12.

International Labour Organization. "Child Labour." http://www.ilo.org/global/topics/child-labour/lang--en/index.htm

IRIN. "Lebanon-Syria: No School Today—Why Syrian Refugee Children Miss Out on Education." August 8, 2012. http://www.irinnews.org/report/96053/lebanon-syria-no-school-today-why-syrian-refugee-children-miss-out-on-education

IRIN. "South Africa: Refugee Children Miss Out on School." January 31, 2012. http://www.irinnews.org/report/94766/south-africa-refugee-children-miss-out-on-school

FURTHER READING

Miller, Larry. "Hidden Homeless." *The Philadelphia Tribune*, July 23, 2010.

Moe, Doug. "Miracle of Education Thriving in Haiti." *Wisconsin State Journal*, November 16, 2012. http://host.madison.com/news/local/doug_moe/doug-moe-miracle-of-education-thriving-in-haiti/article_76df2460-2f8f-11e2-8baa-001a4bcf887a.html

Mozdzer, Jodie. "Array of Science Programs Targets Middle School Girls." *The Courant*, April 7, 2009. http://articles.courant.com/2009-04-07/news/girls-tech-fields0407.art_1_middle-school-girls-all-girl-science-experiences

Osborne, Chad. "Summer Bridge Inspires STEM Education for High School Girls." Radford University, July 15, 2013.

Rashinkar, Nupoor. "School Goes to Children—On Wheels." DNA Syndication, September 22, 2011. http://dnasyndication.com/dna/article/DNIND2821

Right Vision News. "Pakistan: School Merger Deprives Girls of Education." September 12, 2012.

Sauter, Michael B., Alexander E. M. Hess, and Samuel Weigley. "The 10 Poorest Countries in the World." Fox Business, September 14, 2012. http://www.foxbusiness.com/markets/2012/09/14/10-poorest-countries-in-world/

Shadwell, Talia. "Students Share Refugee Experience." *Manawatu Standard*, June 28, 2013. http://www.stuff.co.nz/manawatu-standard/news/8853730/Students-share-refugee-experience

Strauss, Valerie. "US High School Graduation Rate Sees Big Minority Gains—Analysis." *The Washington Post*, June 6, 2013. http://www.washingtonpost.com/blogs/answer-sheet/wp/2013/06/06/u-s-high-school-graduation-rate-sees-big-minority-gains-analysis/

The Times of India. "AMC's School-on-Wheels to Educate Slum Children." August 26, 2011.

UNESCO Institute for Statistics. "Literacy Rate, Adult Female (% of Females Ages 15 and Above)." The World Bank. http://data.worldbank.org/indicator/SE.ADT.LITR.FE.ZS

UN Refugee Agency. "Facts and Figures about Refugees." http://www.unhcr.org.uk/about-us/key-facts-and-figures.html

UN Refugee Agency. "Regional Overview." *Syria Regional Refugee Response*, October 7, 2013. http://data.unhcr.org/syrianrefugees/regional.php

Whitfield, Chandra Thomas. "School Scam." *Crisis*, Spring 2012, Volume 119, Issue 2, p. 22.

GLOSSARY

administrator (ad-MIN-uh-strey-ter) — A person in charge of managing.

corrupt (kuh-RUHPT) — Using dishonest practices.

destitute (DES-ti-toot) — Lacking food, clothing, and shelter.

discriminate (dih-SKRIM-uh-neyt) — To make a judgment for or against a person on the basis of the group, class, or category to which the person belongs.

forensic (fuh-REN-sik) — Pertaining to courts of law.

fundamental (fuhn-duh-MEN-tl) — An essential part of learning, such as reading or writing.

integrate (IN-ti-greyt) — To combine a group of people that were previously separated.

literacy (LIT-er-uh-see) — The ability to read and write.

mainstream (MEYN-streem) — Relating to regular classes or school.

mentor (MEN-tawr) — A person who influences or supports another.

naive (nah-EEV) — Lacking experience or judgment.

peer — A person who is equal to another in age, grade, etc.

progressive (pruh-GRES-iv) — Favoring change, improvement, or reform.

refugee (ref-yoo-JEE) — A person who is forced to flee one's home for safety, usually to another country.

slum — A run-down place where poor people live.

sponsor (SPON-ser) — A person who pays for something on behalf of another.

xenophobia (zen-uh-FOH-bee-uh) — An unreasonable fear or dislike of people from another country.

PHOTO CREDITS: All design elements from Photos.com/Sharon Beck; Cover, p.1—Photos.com; pp. 4, 21, 35— Jupiterimages/Thinkstock; p. 7 —Hector Retamal/AFP/Getty Images/Newscom; p. 8—Master Sgt. Jeremy Lock; p. 11—Ricardo Brazziell/MCT/Newscom; p.12—Mak Remissa/EPA/Newscom; p. 13—Roger L. Wollenberg/UPI/Newscom; p. 15—Charles Lomodong/AFP/Getty Images/Newscom; p. 16—Jamal Nasrallah/EPA/Newscom; p. 19—Girl Scouts of Northern California/Vera Dadok; p. 20—Delores Johnson/KRT/Newscom; p. 23—UK Department for International Development; p. 24—Soeren Stache/dpa/picture-alliance/Newscom; p. 27—Jack Kurtz/ZUMA Press/Newscom; p. 29—Zheng Huansong/Xinhua/Photoshot/Newscom; p. 30—Chrisi1000/Wikimedia; p. 33—Jim Henderson; p. 36—Hazleton Standard-Speaker Ellen F. O'Connell/AP Images; p. 39—Paul Bersebach/ZUMA Press/Newscom; p. 40—Amy Sancetta/AP Images; p. 41—Jim West Image Broker/Newscom.

INDEX

abuse 28
Ahmedabad Municipal Corporation 31
alternative programs 37–38
Amelio, Jamie 9–12
Boli, Laibar 27
bullying 26
Cambodia 9–12
Caring for Cambodia 10–12
Central Connecticut State University 18–19
Central Missouri State University 20
Centre for Education Rights and Transformation 25
Clinton, Bill 7
Clinton Foundation 7
College Board exams 13
Congo, Democratic Republic of the 27
Covenant House 33
discrimination 5, 16, 17, 25–26
Duckenfield, Marty 38
exchange students 13
fees 25–26
Fischer School 39
Fogg, Ally 21
foster care 33
Freyberg High School 27
gender 14, 16–21
Girls in Technology Expo 18–19
GO-GIRL 18
Graced with Orange 11
graduation rates 34, 35
Graves, Earl Jr. 13
Haiti 6–9
Haiti Allies 6, 8–9
Hicks-Groover, Aishia 37–38
Hicks, Johnathan 34, 36–38
Higbie, Sarah 18
Hill, Cordella 33

Holforty, Wendy 19
homelessness 28, 30–31
India 28–32
iTemba Study Centre 24–26
Jain, Bela 32
Jaoude, Miled Abou 22
Jordan 14, 22, 24
kindergarten 38
Kyle, Penelope W. 20
language 6, 13, 14, 22, 26, 27
Lebanon 22–24
literacy rates 14
Lok Vikas Evam Anusandhan Trust 32
Manjoro, Judith 25
marriage 14
mentoring programs 19, 41
Morelus, Guy 9
Morocco 14
Myanmar 27
National Dropout Prevention Center 38
New Zealand 27
Nzamba, Sarah 27
Pakistan 16, 17
Pierre, Miracle 6, 8–9
poverty 5–6, 10, 14, 22, 26, 28–31
preschool 38
Radford University 19–20
Rasid, Paige 18
Reading Recovery 38–39
refugees 15, 22–27
Reiche Elementary 41
Rosch, Joel 38
runaways 28, 30–31, 33
Salaam Baalak Trust 30, 31
Save the Children 22
Savy, Ung 10, 12
Schadt, Daniela 24
Schklair, Ali 41
scholarships 13
school on wheels 31–32

school supplies 10–11, 25, 42
Scott Alternative Learning Center 37–38
Seabrook, Aleyah 18–19
Sharma, Satender 28, 30, 31
Sirchio, Bryan 8
Snow, Kyle 39–40
South Africa 24–26
South Sudan 15
sponsors 8–9
STEM subjects (science, technology, engineering, and math) 18–20
St. Joseph College 18
Sudan 14
summer bridge programs 19–20
Syria 14, 22–24
Taliban 16
Thailand 27
Three2Six 26
Tshili, Antonia 26
United Kingdom 21
United Nations 15, 22, 23, 32
United States 5, 13, 17–20, 33, 34–41
Valle, David 39
Vaughan, David 41
war 5, 14, 15, 22, 23, 27, 34
War Child 23
Waynflete School 41
weapons 36
Williams, Roger 6, 8–9
Women's Influence Network 19
xenophobia 26
Yemen 14
Yousafzai, Malala 16
zero tolerance 34
Zimbabwe 25–26
Zulu, Duduzile 25

About the Author

Tammy Gagne is the author of numerous books for adults and children, including *Life on the Reservations* and *Your Guide to Becoming a US Citizen* for Mitchell Lane Publishers. She resides in northern New England with her husband and son. One of her favorite pastimes is visiting schools to speak to kids about the writing process.